SO-AZA-724

Dear You

MESSAGES FROM YOUR HEART

Jacquelyn B. Fletcher

GOLD HOUSE PRESS
Books and gifts to evolve the human spirit

Illustrations and text © 2014 Jacquelyn B. Fletcher
All rights reserved. Published 2014
Printed in the United States of America

Book and cover design by Cheryl Viker
Editing by Rebecca Rowell
Art photography by Patti Neil
Author photo by Joanna Proesser
Published by Gold House Press
P.O. Box 40, Lakeville, MN 55044
goldhousepress.com

To order in bulk or for wholesale pricing, contact the publisher at info@goldhousepress.com.

ISBN 978-1-941933-00-8 (softcover)

No part of this publication may be reproduced, stored in a retrieval system, or transmitted in
any form or by any means — electronic, mechanical, photocopying, recording, scanning, or
otherwise — without the express written permission of the publisher. Failure to comply with
these terms may expose you to legal action and damages for copyright infringement.

DEDICATION

To my courageous, generous, and
loving heart that continues to show up
day after day after day. Thank you.

TESTIMONIALS

"Jacquelyn's artistry rests in her uncanny ability to make you feel like a long lost friend just walked up and gently tapped you on the shoulder — instantly reminding you of a once easy and essential connection. The presence and clarity of the heart's message is poignant and inescapable."

—Melissa Williamson-Herren, Owner of
Your Art's Desire Gallery of Art and Framing

"Jacquelyn possesses an incredible ability through her art and her words to capture the universal experience of heartache and the sometimes difficult, but always worthwhile, journey of healing. The message of loving and honoring oneself and one's heart is an important message for us all."

—Shannon Barry, MSSW, Executive Director,
Dais: Domestic Abuse Intervention Services

"In Dear You, Jacquelyn Fletcher shares love letters and hopeful whispers from the internal voice we too often ignore. What emerges is a wise, gentle truth that's been too long stifled by our shrill inner critics."

—Pilar Gerasimo, founding editor, *Experience Life* magazine

"Jacquelyn B. Fletcher shares her approach to a heart-filled life in this beautiful, thoughtful, and sincere artwork. If you are in need of connection, healing or inspiration, let the messages from Dear You speak to you."

—Dr. Jan Hoistad, author of *Relationship Rehab* and
Big-Picture Partnering

"I so enjoyed and was moved by the letters in Dear You — searing and soothing all at once."

—Johanna Rian, Ph.D., Mayo Clinic Dolores Jean
Lavins Center for Humanities in Medicine

CONTENTS

Introduction 6
1. Yes 9
2. True 17
3. Valid 25
4. Trust 33
5. Worthy 41
6. Easy 49
7. Brave 57
8. Action 65
9. Support 73
10. Play 81
11. Go! 89
12. Feel 97
13. Connect 105
14. Love 111
15. Spin 119
16. Grateful 125
17. Open 131
18. Listen 139
19. Bold 147
20. Pain 155
21. Help 163
22. Light 171
23. Faith 177
24. Hope 185
25. Yes 193
Acknowledgements 202
About the Author 203

INTRODUCTION

When this world makes us experience pain, it can be so tempting to shut down. Tune out. Close up shop. We vow to never put ourselves out there again. We believe we must protect our hearts by keeping them tightly closed or monitored or quiet. At the first hint of conflict or obstacle or rejection, we crow, "I told you!" And BAM, the gates to our hearts slam shut again.

Not for me. Not anymore.

I don't know about you, but I don't want to live disconnected from my heart. In fact, I want to be in constant communication with it.

My heart is smarter than me.

More intuitive.

More in touch with truth.

After a challenging heartbreak, I wrote these letters to myself addressed from my heart to see if that much-celebrated organ could help me get through the pain. I wondered if listening to my heart could help me gather the wisdom and strength to move on and open up to life again. It could. It did.

At the same time I listened to my heart's council, I created art using acrylic paint and mixed-media techniques to accompany each letter. I placed the art in my workspace and around my home to remind me of my intention to stay connected to my heart. You can find the art at **JacquelynFletcher.com**.

As you read, you might want to write your own messages. Maybe you'll be inspired to create your own art. Go for it!

Research shows that creative expression of any kind — journaling, quilting, writing, painting, singing — can have a positive impact on our health and well-being. I can certainly attest that this project helped me heal.

No matter where you are on your journey, it's time to let your exhausted heart rest. Let your wounded heart recover. Let your loving heart enthusiastically show itself. Your heart knows the way. Trust it as it unfolds.

Here's to your courageous, generous, and loving heart that continues to show up day after day after day.

Love,

Jacque

YES

CHAPTER 1

Dear You,

I'm afraid that someday you'll realize the life we could've had together. Can't we avoid all that?

Love,
Your Heart

Dear You,

you show up. I
show up. It's
that simple.

Love,

Your Heart

Dear You,

STOP! Do you see that? It's so beautiful! Sorry to interrupt. I didn't want you to miss that~

Love,
Your Heart

Dear You,

Let's try it.

Why not?

Love,

Your Heart

Dear You,

The angels are
cheering for you.
Me, too.

Love,
    Your Heart

Dear You,

Come on, you
can do this.
Let. Me In!
Love,
Your Heart

TRUE

CHAPTER 2

Dear You,

Today, I just
need to cry.
Hand me the tissues?
I'll be okay.

Thanks,
        your Heart

Dear You,

You're right.
This hurts like
hell. I'll stay
with you.

Love,

Your Heart

Dear You,

How about a deep breath? Take a big one. Better, right?

Love,

Your Heart

Dear You,

I'm not fearless either, but I'm willing to do what it takes to be whole. Join me?

Love,
Your
Heart

Dea^r] You,

You can always
get | a real job.
I say go for it.

Love,
your Heart

Dear You,

The door will open. Have faith.

Love,
Your
Heart

VALID

CHAPTER 3

Dear You,

You really don't have to hang out with people like that.

Love,
Your Heart

Dear You,

Have you ever considered the fact that even though you're ready, he might not be? Just sayin.'

Love,
Your Heart

Dear You,

You're not an idiot for opening your heart again and again. It's what makes you so beautiful.

Love,
Your Heart

Dear You,

Without these
scars, I wouldn't
be me so stop
trying to hide them.

Love,
Your Heart

Dear You,

Don't let me

be the one who

got away.

Love,

Your Heart

Dear You,

Hearts break and
get sick and give
up every day. Not
yours. Not today.

Love,

Your Heart

TRUST

CHAPTER 4

Dear You

You've left me

behind again.

Again!

Annoyed,

Your Heart

Dear You,

I know I've been a bit hard on you. You don't screw up everything. Can we find a way to work together?

Love,

Your Heart

Dear You,

Let's be BFFs

K?

Love,

Your Heart

Dear You,

Nobody knows me better than you. Nobody.

Love,

Your Heart

Dear you,

The only way you're going to figure this out is to get quiet. Find some water and sit by it.

Love,

Your Heart

Dear You,

It's going to be okay. Really, it is. For now, let's take a break, okay? Why don't you turn on that music you like so much?

Love,

Your Heart

WORTHY

CHAPTER 5

Dear You,

Why are you thinking
so much about the
one negative comment
and no time honoring
the praise you got?
Doesn't make sense.
Love,
Your Heart

Dear You,

Who let the

bully in here?

Turn off that critical

voice this minute.

Love,

Your

Heart

Dear You,

Tell your brain
to stand down!

Love,

Your Heart

Dear You,

If you can't
say anything nice
to yourself, don't
say anything at
all.

Love,
Your Heart

Dear You,

You want proof
you're good enough?
I'm your proof.

Love,

your Heart

Dear You,

If you fail, your dog will still love you. I will too.

Love,

Your Heart

EASY

CHAPTER 6

Dear You,

What's the

rush?

Love,

Your

Heart

Dear You,

I LOVE that I
don't have to
explain myself to
you!

Excited,

Your Heart

Dear You,

Look up!

Love,

Your Heart

Dear You,

Can we schedule
a play date?
Pretty please?

Love,

Your
Heart

Dear You,

Sit down. I mean
it. There's time
for to~dos later.
Please just rest
for a moment.

Thanks,

Your Heart

Dear You,

YAY! I'm so happy you're finally listening to me!

Excited,

Your Heart

BRAVE

CHAPTER 7

Dear You,

Now you've done
it. Lucky for you,
I know how to
handle situations
like this.

Love,

Your Heart

Dear You,

You know there
could be a different
explanation for
the same set of
facts. Think about
it.
Love,
Your Heart

Dear You,

Why don't you
pick up the phone
and let me do
the talking?

Love,

Your Heart

Dear You,

Go say you're
sorry. I'll wait.

Love,
Your
Heart

Dear You,

Stay strong.
I'll help you.

Love,

Your Heart

Dear You,

your passion

is magnetic.

Love,

Your Heart

ACTION

CHAPTER 8

Dear You

Let's do this.

Be brave.

Love,

Your Heart

Dear You,

Let's try a do~
over, okay?
This time, with
heart.

Love,
Your Heart

Dear You,

Let's believe stress
is good for us~
that we can ride
it together like a
rodeo cowboy.
Yeehaw!

Love,
your Heart

Dear You,

We won't be
around forever.
Get to it.

Love,

Your Heart

Dear You,

You can't just sit here wishing.
You know that, right?

Love,
Your Heart

Dear you,

Why are you
keeping the
brakes on?
Confused,

your Heart

SUPPORT

CHAPTER 9

Dear You,

Yep.
Ouch.

On your side,
Your Heart

Dear You,

You stand up for yourself. I'll remind you that those who hurt you are suffering. Deal?

Love,

Your Heart

Dear You,

Who do you think

cleans up the

messes you make?
Please don't turn
your back on me.

Hurting,

Your Heart

Dear You,

I'll always give
you another chance.
Always.

Love,

Your Heart

Dear You,

you are
strong enough.

Love,
Your Heart

Dear You,

Let go ~

I got this.

Love,

Your Heart

PLAY

CHAPTER 10

Dear You,

Would you please
lighten up? I
could use a
laugh or two.

Love,

Your Heart

Dear You,

Get your ass

to yoga.

Love,

Your Heart

Dear You,

Yes! Feel this!

Feel it all.

Love,

Your Heart

Dear You,

Right on! I love
it when you
get me pumping
fast.

Love,

Your Heart

Dear You,

God, that was good. Let's do that again.

Love,

Your Heart

Dear You,

Have you asked
yourself what
your heart would
say?

Love,
     Your Heart

GO !

CHAPTER 11

Dear You,

Why do you have
to figure it out?
Can't we just go
for the ride this
time?
Love,
Your Heart

Dear You,

I get that you're
scared. But if you
dont share me soon,
I'm going to start
causing trouble.

Love,

Your Heart

Dear You,

You can trust
this. It's real.

Love,

Your Heart

Dear You,

could you please
grow a set?

Exasperated,

Your Heart

Dear You,

Keep trying.

Keep going.

Keep the faith.
I am.

Love,
Your Heart

Dear You,

I dare you~

Love,

Your Heart

FEEL

CHAPTER 12

Dear You,

Every time you whine about being all alone it hurts me. Am I not enough for you?

Love,
Your Heart

Dear You,

I'm sorry you
feel that way.
I'm not sorry
I showed up.
Love,
Your Heart

Dear You,

What's the
hurry?

Tired,

Your Heart]

Dear You,

Yes, I'm emotional.
What's wrong with
that?

Love,

Your Heart

Dear You,

Nobody is coming
to save you
but me!

Irritated,

Your Heart

Dear You,

All right! I'm

done pouting.

Love,

Your Heart

CONNECT

CHAPTER 13

Dear You,

Thank you for having such amazing friends. I need them right now.

Love,

Your Heart

Dear You,

What's so hard
about asking
for help?

Confused,

Your Heart

Dear you,

 I know it feels

like you're all
alone. Why don't
you reach out to
someone you love?"

 Love,
    Your Heart

Dear You,

Those people who love you save your life every day.

Love,

Your Heart

LOVE

CHAPTER 14

Dear You,

What's so scary
about love?
Seriously. I don't
get it.
Love,
your Heart

Dear You,

He's the one!
I know it!!

Love,

Your Heart

Dear you,

She loves you.

You know that, right?

Love,

Your Heart

Dear You,

I don't care if you think love is cheesy. I'll take more cheese, please.

Love,

Your Heart

Dear You,

Here's what I love about you~
love about you~
everything!

Love,

Your Heart

Dear You,

Don't you want
to spend all
your time feeling
this good?

Love,
        Your Heart

SPIN

CHAPTER 15

Dear You,

What's with all
the drama?

Love,
Your Heart

Dear You,

You're spinning
your wheels. Let's
go for a walk and
think about something
else for a while.

Thanks,
   Your Heart

Dear You,

You're the reason

this keeps on
happening

Patiently,

Your Heart

Dear You,

Pay attention.

Please.

Love,

Your Heart

GRATEFUL

CHAPTER 16

Dear You,

This life is

pretty amazing.

Don't you think?

Love,

Your Heart

Dear You,

I am so AWESOME,
which means you
are, too.

Love,
    your Heart

Dear You,

Let's give
something to
someone today.
You in?

Love,
your Heart

Dear You,

Thank you,
thank you,
THANK YOU!

Love,

Your Heart

OPEN

CHAPTER 「17」

Dear You,

Oh, honey, don't you get it? Without me, you have nothing Can't we resolve this?

Love you no matter what,
Your Heart

Dear You,

You say you want
to live with an
open heart. Then
why are you constantly
closing my door?

Concerned,
Your Heart

Dear You,

It's freezing in here. What's missing? Oh, yes, ME.

Exasperated,
your Heart

Dear You,

Please don't
shut me
out~

Love,
Your Heart

Dear You,

I'll tell you what you deserve~ a loving, peaceful heart. I'm yours if you want me.

Love,
Your Heart

Dear You,

No matter what
happens, I'm
with you until
the end.

Love,

Your Heart

LISTEN

CHAPTER 18

Dear You,

I will never

shut up. Ever!

Love,

your Heart

Dear You,

Wake me up when
you're done
sabotaging yourself
for the millionth
time.

Tiredly,

Your Heart

Dear You,

'quick question~
why do you keep
doing that when
you know it's not
good for you?

Love,
        Your Heart

Dear You,

Why are you always last on your list?

Love,

Your Heart

Dear You,

I vow to give

you hope whenever

you need it.

Love,

Your Heart

Dear You,

Haven't you learned
by now that I'm an
asset not | a liability?

Irritated,

Your Heart !

BOLD

CHAPTER 19

Dear You,

Since when does
everyone else's
opinion matter
more than your
own?

Confused,
Your Heart

Dear You,

Who are you
going to believe?
Them? Or me?
Love,
Your Heart

Dear You,

What if it
isn't true?

Love,

Your Heart

Dear You,

You're not a fraud.
You're talented.
And what's more,
you've got heart.

Love,

Your Heart

Dear You,

Please don't keep
me all to yourself.

Love,

Your Heart

Dear You,

I'm yours. Where

do I sign?

Love you,

Your Heart

PAIN

CHAPTER 20

Dear You,

I'm so sorry.

Love you,

Your Heart|

Dear You,

This sucks. Let's face it, together so we can move on. Agreed?

Love,

Your Heart

Dear You,

We'll figure
this out.

Love,

Your Heart

Dear You,

You need me

just as much as

I need you.

Love

Your Heart

Dear You,

I'm still

beating.

Love,

Your Heart

Dear You,

I know you can

be a warrior when
you need to be.
How about being a
warrior with heart?

Love,
Your Heart

HELP

CHAPTER 21

Dear You,

Can't this wait
until tomorrow?
You'll feel better
after some sleep.
Promise.

Love,
    Your Heart

Dear You,

I know, and you
know, you know.

Love,

Your Heart

Dear You,

Who taught you to
believe this crap?
Trust me, you're
worth it.

Love,

Your Heart

Dear You,

I refuse to justify myself to you.

Love,

Your Heart

Dear You,

I've got your
back, remember?

Love,
Your Heart

Dear You,

Quit talking.
Start being.
Please.

Love,
Your Heart |

LIGHT

CHAPTER 22

Dear You

I'm scared, too.

Turn on a light?
It will help.

Love,

Your Heart

Dear You,

I'm not perfect, but at least I'm willing to stand in the fire with You. You could learn from my example.

Tired,

Your Heart

D ear You,

I want to go
there, I do.
Just give me a
minute, okay?

Love,

Your Heart

Dear You,

I trust you.

Love,

Your Heart

FAITH

CHAPTER 23

Dear You,

It's time for

a leap of faith.

I'll jump with

you.

Love,

your Heart

Dear You,

Why not surround yourself with beloveds who help you shine even brighter?

Love,

Your Heart

Dear You,

You're a kindhearted sweetheart with a heart of gold. I should know.

Love,

Your Heart

Dear You,

You didn't do anything wrong.

Love,

Your Heart

Dear You,
you know you
always land on
your feet. Why not
give it a shot?

Love,
    your Heart

Dear You,

Believe it.

Love,

Your Heart

HOPE

CHAPTER 24

Dear You,

That smile?
I made you do
that. You're
welcome.

Love,

   Your Heart

Dear You,

I'll make a
memory of this
moment so you
can take it out
and look at it
anytime you want.

Love,
Your Heart

Dear You,

Don't you see?
You are my soul
mate.

Love,

Your Heart

Dear You,

I know my
enthusiasm makes
you nervous. Too bad!
I'm all in. For good.

Love,

Your Heart

Dear You,

I can take care of
myself. You just
keep saying YES and
let me worry about
myself, okay?
Go on. say yes.

Love,
    Your Heart

Dear You,

You have my

blessing.

Love

Your Heart

YES

CHAPTER 25

Dear You,

Thank you, brave soul, for your willingness to keep showing up.

Love,

Your Heart

Dear You,

I am so proud
of you. I know
what it took for
you to do this.
Bravo!

Admiringly,
Your Heart

Dear You,

This feels so good. Can we do this more often?

Love,

Your Heart

Dear You,

I love you,

forever and ever,
always.

Love,

Your Heart

Dear You,

The more you

offer me up,

the stronger

I get.

Love,

Your Heart

Dear You,

Be ALL of who
you are, 'cause
you're awesome.

Love,
Your Heart

Dear You,

Say yes.

Love,

Your Heart

Acknowledgements

My heart is packed full of love for the teachers, kindred spirits, and beloved souls who have showed me how to connect with my heart. Thanks so much to you all. This book was born out of heartbreak and proved to me that the heart is the most adaptive, creative, and courageous organ of all. I am deeply grateful to my daughter, Evangeline, who answered my lament, "Who is going to turn my words into art?" with the most obvious answer: "I will, Mama!" My brother, John, said, "Your words are art." And the lovely Rachel Awes proved I could make my own art.

My husband, Arne, signed up to walk beside me, and I am so happy he did. He provides me with support in more ways than he can ever really know. He put up with art all over every surface of our house while I experimented.

My soul sisters, Lynn Devlin, Maggie Knoke, and Heidi Pederson contributed feedback and editorial direction that was critical to this project. A big thank you to Rebecca Rowell, who provides amazing copyediting and heartfelt cheerleading on all of my projects. To Cheryl Viker, who designed these pages and who puts up with my enthusiasm and matches it with her own drive to get 'er done. To Melissa and Ken Herren, the owners of Your Art's Desire Gallery who generously gave their hearts and smarts to this project. And to Patti Neil for photographing all my artwork for this book.

To the creative spirits who cheer me on and contribute their ideas, support, time, and encouragement: Dottie Bacon, Jennifer Dodgson, Brian Donahue, Andréa Gerasimo, Pilar Gerasimo, Tracy Glenz, Jocelyn Hale, Jan Hoistad, Jean Travis Odefey, Johanna Rian, Susan Riley, Jan Senn, Tracy Sides, Sarah Spencer, and Stephanie Watson.

And finally, to all the people who've broken my heart over the years. Without you all, this book and the wisdom it contains wouldn't exist.

ABOUT THE AUTHOR

 Jacquelyn B. Fletcher is an award-winning author and speaker. She's co-creator and host of the Healing Words television show and a founding faculty member of the Creative Writing at the Bedside program, both administered by the Mayo Clinic Dolores Jean Lavins Center for Humanities in Medicine in Rochester, Minnesota. Really, she's a transformation expert. She's lost 100 pounds and kept it off for nearly 20 years. Dug herself out of debt. And recovered from a broken heart again and again.

Her books and projects all aim to support healing, encourage empowerment, and inspire transformation.

To check out the collection of Dear You art and gifts, or to find out about having Jacquelyn speak to your group, visit **JacquelynFletcher.com**.

CPSIA information can be obtained
at www.ICGtesting.com
Printed in the USA
FFOW05n1738100416